Imaginations 2

Relaxation Stories & Guided Imagery FOR KIDS

By Carolyn Clarke

This book is dedicated to my husband.

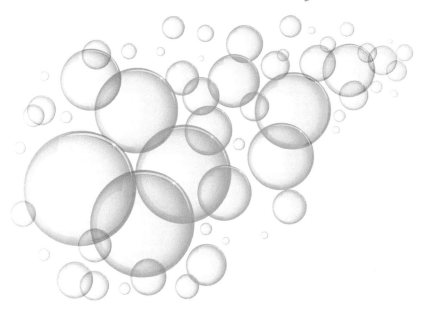

ISBN-10: 0990732207
ISBN-13: 978-0-9907322-0-4

Library of Congress Control Number: 2014947952

PRINTED IN THE UNITED STATES OF AMERICA

Table of Contents

Information for Adults 1

Yoga Prep Poses and Breathing Games.............................. 7

Introduction for Kids 13

Relaxation Stories 15

    Tight and Soft 17

    A Fall Day 18

    Wintertime 21

    Springtime 22

    Summertime 25

    Rainbow Flower Garden.. 26

    The Thunder Drum 29

    The End of the Rainbow 30

    Nighttime Animal Adventure 33

    Lavender Fields 34

    Rainbow Bubbles 37

    Butterflies 38

    Mandalas 41

    Sunset 42

    Dinosaur Friend 45

    In the Desert 46

    Making Chocolate 49

    More Loving Kindness 50

Additional Information and Resources................................ 52

Acknowledgements 53

Information for Adults

This book contains whimsical children's stories filled with guided imagery designed to guide the listener to a peaceful place with lots of sensory descriptions. By imagining the sights, sounds, smells, feelings, and even tastes of a peaceful place, readers can convince their brains that their bodies are actually there. Guided imagery can feel like a mini-vacation because it calms the body and focuses the mind. As you've probably noticed, for most children, engaging with their imaginations is effortless, so guided imagery is particularly effective at teaching children to relax. And, of course, children love to be read to.

I have used the short and sweet relaxation stories included in this book in my children's yoga classes since 2002. My students arrive bouncing with energy. We stretch, move, and breathe with yoga poses. At the end of the class, I read them a story filled with guided imagery. I watch them become more still, quiet, and relaxed with each word. Sometimes, they even drift off to sleep. The kids often tell me that the relaxation story is their favorite part of the class.

Below is a sample of one of the stories included in this book. It is helpful to experience an example of guided imagery prior to using it with the children in your life. As you read it, notice if you feel any released tension in your body. Also, many adults find it more effective to listen to guided imagery, so I would recommend asking someone else to read this story to you.

Butterflies

Imagine that you are lying in a field of grass.

Look up at the blue sky and fluffy, white clouds.

Now imagine a colorful butterfly flying above you.

All of the colors of the rainbow decorate its wings.

Now imagine another butterfly flying above you.

Look at all the colors of this butterfly's wings.

Imagine that more and more butterflies are
flying over you.

Each one is colorful and beautiful in its own way.

The sky is now filled with butterflies.

Listen to the soft sound of their fluttering wings.

Imagine that they gently move the air around you.

You can feel the breeze from the butterflies on your body.

When the air touches your body, it helps you relax.

Feel the air on your feet.

And feel your feet relax.

Now feel the air on your legs.

Feel your legs relax.

Feel the breeze from the butterflies on your belly.

Feel your belly relax.

Feel the air on your arms.

Feel your arms relax.

Feel the air on your face.

Feel your face relax.

Your whole body is relaxed and calm.

Enjoy lying in the grass, watching the butterflies
until they fly away.

Do you feel calmer after reading this story? The children in your life will also feel relaxed after experiencing it. Kids need time to wind down after busy and hectic days. Children may struggle with the morning routine of waking, dressing, eating breakfast, gathering up their things, and getting out the door. At school, they are busy for hours, learning and socializing, often in a very structured environment. They may even take a test or two. Afterschool activities give way to homework time, dinner time, bath time, and then bedtime. Time to relax is easily lost in the shuffle. However, the benefits of taking time to relax are just as important as anything else in their daily routines.

Benefits of Relaxation

Reduction in stress

Lower heart rate and blood pressure

Less muscle tension

Improved concentration and focus

Increased ability to learn

Weight loss

Behavioral improvements

Better sleep

Relaxation can help with:

Anxiety before school, a test, or a big event

Sleep disorders, nightmares,
or being afraid of the dark

Autism, ADD, ADHD

Depression

Low self—esteem or negativity

Life changes such as moving, divorce,
death in the family, or going to new schools

Excessive worrying

When to Use a Relaxation Story

At home

Before school   After school

At bedtime

At school

Before class   After recess

Before a test   On a rainy day

Before creative writing or art projects

At play

During children's yoga   Before a sporting event

Before a music or dance recital

While traveling   For fun

Before arts and crafts

Before writing in a journal

Imagine children hearing short, sweet relaxation
stories throughout their day. After a short story before
school, the morning routine might not be a struggle any longer.
Once they are at school, children who hear a story that engages all five senses
are better able to focus and concentrate. Their classroom behavior and grades might
even improve. At home, guided imagery at bedtime can help with sleep problems that
keep children from drifting happily off to sleep.

When using this book, read a single story or a few at a time in a soft, soothing, and slow
voice. Remember to give the child enough time to not only hear your words, but also
process and imagine them before you read the next line of the story. If you have time for
a long relaxation session, begin with the breathing games and yoga prep poses on the
following pages prior to reading a relaxation story. These exercises help the child settle
even quicker and deeper into a calm state. Then read the first story, "Tight and Soft,"
which is based on the practice of progressive muscle relaxation and helps the body relax even more deeply. Finally, choose any of the following, more vivid and imaginative
stories. If you are in a hurry, reading even just one short story will be beneficial.

To make relaxation time even more special, try using a relaxation prop. Diffuse essential
oils known to increase relaxation, like lavender, chamomile, or ylang ylang, into the room
or inhale their scent directly from the bottle during story time. Eye pillows filled with flax
seeds and lavender flowers are soothing to the eyes and face and help children's minds
reach inward. Be mindful, though, that what works for one child might not work for another. Children with sensitivities or special needs may not find these props relaxing, and
it is always important to check for allergies before using any oils or scents.

If your children and students love these stories—and I think they will—you can always
find more in my first book, *Imaginations: Fun Relaxation Stories and Meditations for Kids*.
Audio versions read aloud by me are also available at www.ImaginationsForKids.com,
where you'll find extension activities that correspond with each story. I've been told
that there are enough ideas to keep you busy for months!

I hope that this book is helpful and creates many fun and restful experiences
for both you and the children in your life.

Happy Relaxing,
Carolyn

Yoga Prep Poses and Breathing Games

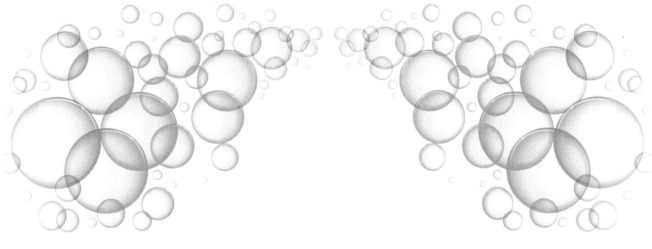

NOTE: Yoga and breathing can be used to prepare children for the relaxation stories. I use these poses and breathing games in my yoga classes to transition from active time to relaxation time. Breathing exercises help calm the body by focusing the mind on the breath. The yoga poses are slow and calming exercises that are all done while lying on the back. This position is ideal because it activates the part of the nervous system responsible for the body's relaxation response (the parasympathetic nervous system). Lying down for yoga also keeps the child grounded in one place instead of allowing him or her to roam around. Plus, the eyes naturally go to the ceiling instead of around the room, helping the child focus.

Here are a few fun yoga poses and breathing games that complement any relaxation story in this book:

Breathing Games

Hoberman Sphere

A Hoberman Sphere is a colorful science toy that is also a great visual tool for breathing exercises. Visit BambinoYoga.com for purchasing info.

Hold the Hoberman Sphere in your hands or let it rest on the ground.

Open it slowly and breathe in.

Close it slowly and breathe out.

Keep opening and closing it with your breath.

Fun!

Heart Breath

Breathe in and open your arms out to the sides like a T.

Breathe out and put your hands over your heart.

Stay in this position for a minute.

Do it again!

Sound Breaths

Yawning

Take a deep breath in, and as you breathe out, yawn and say, "Ahhhhhhh."

Feel your face, shoulders, and neck relax.

Humming

Take a deep breath in. Keeping your mouth closed, breathe out and say "Mmmmmmm."

Make this humming sound two more times.

Buzzing Bee

Take a deep breath in and say, "Zzzzzzzzzzzzzzzzzzzzzzzzzzzz," as you breathe out.

You'll sound like a buzzing bee! Try it one more time.

Yoga Poses

Knee Hug

1. Lie down on the ground or on your bed.

2. Bring your knees to your chest.

3. Wrap your arms around your knees as if you're giving yourself a big hug.

Happy Baby

1. From Knee Hug, let go of your legs.

2. Keep your knees bent, and reach your feet up into the air.

3. Reach up with your arms, and hold on to the bottoms of your feet.

Legs Up

1. From Happy Baby, let go of your feet.

2. Reach your legs straight up in the air.

3. This pose can also be done with your legs resting on a wall.

Starfish (or "Savasana")

1. From Legs Up, bring your legs down to the ground.

2. Leave a little space between your feet.

3. Lay your arms along the sides of your body, with your palms facing up to the sky.

Introduction for Kids

Yippee! It's time to relax.

Have you had a long day at school and need a little down time?

Are you feeling cranky, worried, or sad about something that happened today?

Or do you feel good, and you want to feel even better?

Relaxing our bodies and focusing our minds helps us to feel happy and healthy.

Have fun imagining the stories in this book!

Each one is an adventure that can take you to magical places.

You'll have a chance to:

- Take a nap with a dinosaur!

- Travel the world and say goodnight to animals!

- Follow a rainbow to its end!

- Hike in the desert!

- Relax in summer, spring, fall, and winter!

- And lots more!

Ask an adult or friend to read a story to you, and enjoy feeling peaceful and calm.

Have fun and happy relaxing!

Carolyn

Relaxation Stories

Tight and Soft

NOTE: This story is based on progressive muscle relaxation, which helps a child's body settle into listening and imagining. Try reading this story before any of the others in this book.

Lie down on your back.

Stretch out your legs on the ground with a little space between your feet.

Lay your arms along the sides of your body, with your palms facing up to the sky.

Now you are going to help your body be relaxed and calm.

First, squeeze the muscles in your toes and feet.

Make them tight.

Now make your toes soft and relaxed.

Squeeze the muscles in your legs.

Make them tight.

Now make your legs soft and relaxed.

Squeeze your tummy.

Make it tight.

Now make your tummy soft and relaxed.

Squeeze your arms and make a fist.

Make them tight.

Now make your arms and hands soft and relaxed.

Squeeze your face.

Make it tight, like a raisin face.

Now make your face soft and relaxed.

Squeeze your whole body.

Make your whole body tight.

Now make your whole body soft and relaxed.

A Fall Day

Imagine it is the first day of fall.

Go for a walk and notice the cool feeling of the air.

Imagine that you see a squirrel gathering nuts.

You hear the sound of birds off in the distance.

You see a flock of geese flying south, to warmer weather.

Now imagine that you see the most colorful tree you've ever seen.

Walk up to the tree and hear the crunch of the leaves under your feet.

Lie down under the tree.

Feel the leaves under your body.

Take a deep breath and see if you can smell the leaves.

Look up at the leaves that are still on the tree.

Can you see the blue sky through them?

Picture all the colors of the leaves.

Red, orange, yellow, and purple.

Imagine that the wind gently blows a few leaves off the tree.

Watch them fall slowly and land softly on the ground.

Now imagine that the leaves start to fall onto you.

They cover you in a relaxing and cozy leaf blanket.

Imagine that red leaves fall on your feet and your feet relax.

Orange leaves fall on your legs, and your legs relax.

Yellow leaves fall on your belly, and your belly relaxes.

Purple leaves fall on your arms and hands, and they relax, too.

Enjoy how relaxed your whole body feels.

Lie here under your colorful leaf blanket, enjoying this fall day.

Wintertime

Imagine it is the first day of winter.

You have on a snowsuit, mittens, a hat, and boots that keep you very warm.

Only your cheeks and nose can feel the cold winter air.

Imagine playing in the snow.

You could build a snowman or dig a giant hole.

Now imagine lying down on the snow.

You still feel very warm and cozy in your snowsuit.

It starts to snow.

Stick out your tongue and taste the snow.

Can you hear the sound of the snowflakes falling to the ground?

Look up and see all of the snowflakes in the sky.

Look closely and see how each one looks different and beautiful, just like you.

Imagine that the snow falling on your body helps you relax.

Feel the snowflakes fall on your feet, and feel your feet relax.

Feel the snowflakes fall on your legs, and feel your legs relax.

Feel the snowflakes fall on your belly, and feel your belly relax.

Feel the snowflakes fall on your arms and hands, and feel them relax.

Feel a few snowflakes fall on your face, and feel your face relax, too.

Let your body stay very still in the snow.

Now imagine that you are an animal that hibernates in the winter.

Maybe you are a squirrel, a groundhog, or even a bear.

Feel your animal fur keeping you warm. Let your body be very still.

Take slow breaths in and out.

In and out. In and out.

Like a hibernating animal, rest and relax all winter long.

Springtime

Imagine that it is the first day of spring.

The sun comes out and melts the snow on the ground.

Imagine the snow getting softer and softer, mushier and mushier.

Now feel the warmth of the sun on your body.

Feel your body getting softer, like the snow.

Your feet soften and relax.

Your legs soften and relax.

Your belly softens and relaxes.

Your arms and hands soften and relax, too.

Your face softens and relaxes.

Imagine that your whole body softens and relaxes, like a puddle of melted snow.

Now the puddle soaks into the ground.

The water reaches hundreds of tiny wildflower seeds waiting in the soil.

The seeds soak in the water and begin to grow.

Imagine that a tiny green bud sprouts from each of the seeds.

They grow, inch by inch, out of the soil.

Higher.

Higher.

And higher.

Leaves and flower buds sprout from the plant.

Imagine the flower buds opening into beautiful colorful blossoms.

Take a deep breath in to smell the flowers. Then let it out.

And take another deep breath, in and out, smelling the flowers.

And one more breath in and out.

Enjoy being surrounded by flowers on this relaxing spring day.

Summertime

Imagine that it's the first day of summer and the longest day of the year.

The sun is bright and hot, and you are at the beach.

You have a colorful raft to float on.

Take a deep breath in, and then blow out, filling the raft with air.

Take another deep breath. Then blow out again, making the raft bigger.

Take one more deep breath, and then blow out, filling up the raft.

You are very hot and feel like going for a swim.

You slowly go out into the cool, calm water with your raft.

Holding on to your raft, float in the water and look at all you can see from here.

Palm trees bend slowly with the wind, and there's a colorful rainbow off in the distance.

Take a deep breath in and smell coconut sunscreen and sweet-smelling tropical flowers.

Run your tongue over your lips and see if you can taste the salt in the air, too.

Listen to the sound of the waves on the shore.

Do you hear seagulls or other kids laughing?

Imagine that you climb onto the raft and float on your back.

Feel the water gently rock you back and forth as you float.

The cool ocean breeze on your wet skin relaxes each part of your body.

Feel the breeze on your feet, and feel them relax.

Feel the breeze on your legs, and feel them relax.

Feel the breeze on your belly, and feel your belly relax.

Feel the breeze on your arms and hands, and feel them relax, too.

Now feel the breeze on your face.

Smile and then let your face relax.

Cool and calm, enjoy floating and relaxing on this summer day.

Rainbow Flower Garden

Lie down on your back.

Imagine that you are a flower garden.

Each bone in your back is a seed.

The rest of your body is soil that covers the seeds.

Imagine that rain starts to fall and waters your seeds.

Watch the seeds as they sprout from the soil.

Tiny buds appear, and the flowers in your garden begin to bloom.

As each flower blossoms, your body relaxes.

Red roses bloom at the bottom of your spine.

Feel your back relax.

Orange sunflowers grow at your belly button.

Feel your belly relax.

Yellow buttercups grow above your belly button.

Feel your back relax even more.

Green grass grows from your chest and heart.

Feel your chest and heart relax.

Blueberries grow near your throat.

Feel your neck and throat relax.

A lavender flower grows in between your eyebrows, and your whole face relaxes.

Now imagine that one beautiful purple lotus flower blooms from the top of your head.

Your whole body feels relaxed and soft.

Take a deep breath in and out to smell the flowers in your garden.

The rainbow colors of your flowers shine like twinkling and sparkling lights.

You are as beautiful as this bright and colorful flower garden.

The Thunder Drum

Imagine you are lying in your bed.

It's nighttime, and it begins to rain.

You can hear the sound of raindrops hitting the windows.

They start slowly,

And get faster,

And faster,

And faster.

You hear the sound of thunder off in the distance.

It sounds like someone playing a giant drum in the sky.

Imagine that the sound of the thunder drum helps your body relax.

Each time the thunder drum booms, your body gets softer and more relaxed.

The thunder drum booms, and your feet relax.

The thunder drum booms, and your legs relax.

The thunder drum booms, and your belly relaxes.

The thunder drum booms, and your hands and arms relax.

The thunder drum booms, and your face relaxes.

The drum gets softer and softer, until you can't hear it anymore.

Listen to the sound of the raindrops.

The rain begins to slow down.

The raindrops get slower,

And slower,

And slower.

Feel how relaxed your body is after the rainstorm.

The End of the Rainbow

Imagine that you are lying in a field of grass.

Let your body relax and get very heavy, letting the ground hold you.

Now imagine that it starts to rain.

The raindrops that fall from the sky are just the right temperature—
not too cold and not too warm.

Imagine that as the raindrops fall on your body, they help you relax even more.

Feel the raindrops falling on your toes and feet.

Feel them relax.

Now feel the rain on your legs, and let them relax.

Feel the rain on your belly.

And feel the rain falling on your arms, your hands, and your fingertips.

Feel each body part relax.

The rain falls on your head and face.

Each raindrop washes away any fear or worries that you have.

Feel your whole body become relaxed and calm.

The rain slowly stops, and a beautiful rainbow appears in the sky.

Look at all the colors of the rainbow:

Red…orange…yellow…green…blue…indigo…and purple.

Imagine that you follow the rainbow until it ends.

What do you see?

Green rolling hills?

A pot of gold, shimmering in the sunlight?

Maybe even a dancing leprechaun, wearing green?

Now imagine that you follow the rainbow back to your resting spot in the grass.

Watch the rainbow until the colors slowly fade away.

Enjoy how relaxed and calm your body feels.

Nighttime Animal Adventure

Imagine that you are going to fly around the world to see animals.

Picture how you will do this.

It could be by plane, in a helicopter, or even on a flying carpet.

Perhaps you have your own wings for flying.

Now imagine that you take off and begin to fly.

Look down and see all the animals that live on the planet.

As you fly over Africa, you see giraffes, rhinos, and elephants.

You even see hippos and lions.

It's nighttime, and they are going to sleep.

Watch the lions yawn.

Imagine you yawn, too, and you say goodnight to the animals.

Now imagine that you fly to another place in the world.

Imagine the animals that you see there.

Wild boar and deer in Europe?

Kangaroos and koalas in Australia?

Sea turtles and parrots in South America?

Pandas and tigers in Asia?

Bald eagles and monarch butterflies in North America?

Imagine that all the animals you see are getting ready to sleep.

Seeing the sleepy animals makes you feel very tired, too.

Imagine flying back to your home and landing in your bed.

Your body feels relaxed, calm, and sleepy,
just like the animals all around the world.

Lavender Fields

NOTE: Try using this story with lavender essential oil to experience the calming scent of a lavender field. Lavender essential oil also promotes a restful sleep.

Imagine that you are walking in a field full of lavender flowers.

There are rows of these tall purple flowers as far as you can see.

You can hear bees buzzing as they gather pollen from the lavender.

Imagine colorful butterflies landing on the flowers all around you.

Now imagine that you find the perfect spot in the lavender field.

Lie down. Then take a deep breath in and out.

Smell the lavender all around you.

The perfume of the lavender helps your body relax and makes you sleepy.

Breathe in and out.

Feel your feet relax.

Breathe in and out.

Feel your legs relax.

Breathe in and out.

Feel your belly relax.

Breathe in and out.

Feel your arms relax.

Breathe in and out.

Feel your face relax.

Breathe in and out.

Feel your whole body relax.

Rest and relax here in the field while you enjoy the smell of the lavender flowers.

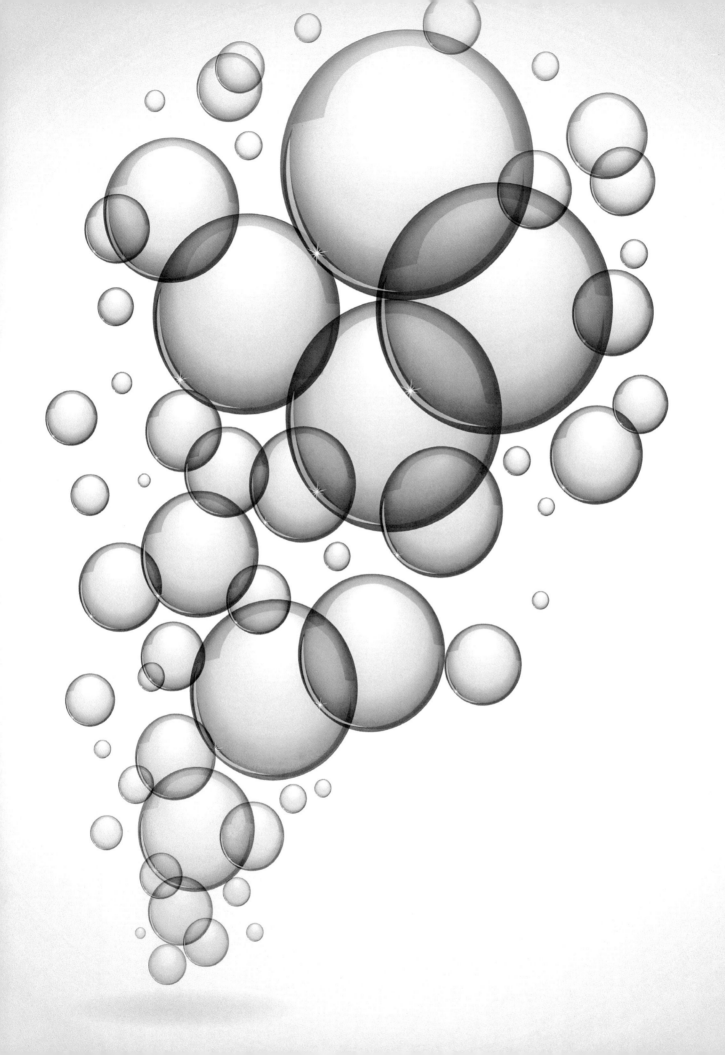

Rainbow Bubbles

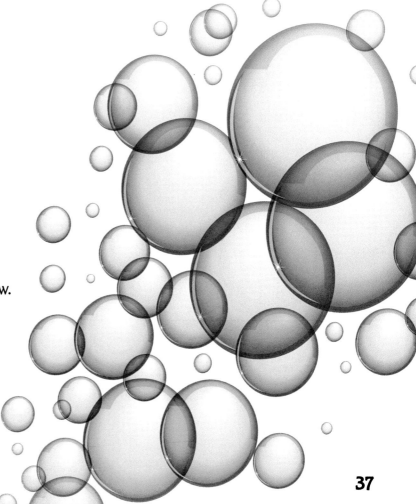

Imagine that you can blow bubbles.

Every time you breathe out, colorful bubbles blow from your mouth.

Take a deep breath in.

Blow out a bubble that's your favorite color.

Watch it float away.

Take another deep breath.

Breathe out, blowing lots of colorful bubbles into the air.

Watch the bubbles floating above you, dancing in the air.

Now breathe in.

Blow out red bubbles.

Breathe in.

Blow out orange bubbles.

Breathe in.

Blow out yellow bubbles.

Breathe in.

Blow out green bubbles.

Breathe in.

Blow out blue bubbles.

Breathe in.

Blow out purple bubbles.

A rainbow of bubbles floats above you now.

Watch each bubble until it floats away.

Butterflies

Imagine that you are lying in a field of grass.

Look up at the blue sky and fluffy, white clouds.

Now imagine a colorful butterfly flying above you.

All of the colors of the rainbow decorate its wings.

Now imagine another butterfly flying above you.

Look at all the colors of this butterfly's wings.

Imagine that more and more butterflies are flying over you.

Each one is colorful and beautiful in its own way.

The sky is now filled with butterflies.

Listen to the soft sound of their fluttering wings.

Imagine that they gently move the air around you.

You can feel the breeze from the butterflies on your body.

When the air touches your body, it helps you relax.

Feel the air on your feet.

And feel your feet relax.

Now feel the air on your legs.

Feel your legs relax.

Feel the breeze from the butterflies on your belly.

Feel your belly relax.

Feel the air on your arms.

Feel your arms relax.

Feel the air on your face.

Feel your face relax.

Your whole body is relaxed and calm.

Enjoy lying in the grass, watching the butterflies until they fly away.

Mandalas

NOTE: The word mandala (**man**-duh-luh) means "circle" in Sanskrit. Focusing on the center of the repeating mandala pattern can help you relax and concentrate. Mandalas are often found in nature in the form of things like sand dollars, spiderwebs, and sunflowers.

Imagine that you see a sand dollar.

A sand dollar is a mandala.

You see a star shape in the center of the sand dollar.

Looking at the star, take a deep breath in and out.

Trace the outside of the sand dollar with your eyes.

Now imagine that you see a spiderweb.

A spiderweb is a mandala, too.

Feeling very safe, you see a spider at the center of the web.

Looking at the spider, take a deep breath in and out.

Trace the circle around the outside of the spiderweb with your eyes.

Now imagine that you see a sunflower.

A sunflower is a mandala, too.

Look at the brown center of the sunflower.

Take a deep breath in and out, smelling the center of the sunflower.

Now look at all the yellow petals.

Count the number of petals that you see.

Starting with the top petal, count the petals around the circle.

Now imagine drawing your own mandala.

Take out your imaginary crayons and draw a circle.

Looking at the center of your mandala,
take a deep breath in and out.

Now imagine drawing petals around your circle.

Enjoy the beautiful mandala that you have drawn.

Feel how relaxed you are when you imagine mandalas.

Sunset

Imagine that you are at the beach.

Look at the blue sky and the fluffy white clouds.

Listen to the sound of the waves on the shore.

Now find the sun in the sky.

Close your eyes and feel the warmth of the sun on your face.

Breathe in and breathe out.

The warmth of the sun relaxes your face.

Find the sun in the sky again.

It has moved lower in the sky and closer to the water.

Breathe in and breathe out again.

The warm sun relaxes your arms.

Find the sun in the sky now.

It has moved even lower.

Now breathe in and out.

Feel the sun relaxing your belly.

Find the sun even lower in the sky.

Breathe in and breathe out.

Feel the sun relaxing your legs and feet.

Watch the sun become bright red as it gets closer to the water.

The sky and clouds light up in red, pink, and orange colors.

Imagine that the water is like a mirror for the sunset.

You can see the same colors in the sky and the water.

Watch the sun slowly disappear,
bringing morning sunshine to the other side of the world.

Relax and enjoy the beautiful painting the sun has drawn in the sky for you.

Dinosaur Friend

Imagine that you can travel back in time to see the dinosaurs.

Get in your time-travel machine.

Buckle your seat belt.

Countdown to takeoff.

10…9…8…7…6…5…4…3…2…1…Go!

Imagine that you travel back in time.

Get out of your time-travel machine and start to explore.

Imagine that you see a dinosaur with a long neck, eating leaves from a tree.

You feel very safe because the dinosaur is friendly.

Imagine walking closer.

The dinosaur is huge!

He sees you and brings his head down to say hello.

Feeling very safe, you look into the dinosaur's eyes.

He smiles at you, and you smile at him.

You can hear him breathing in and out, just like you.

Now imagine that he lies down next to you for a nap.

He lets you climb on top of him and rest on his belly.

Now you can feel him breathing.

When he breaths in, you move up. When he breaths out, you move down.

Up and down.

Up and down.

Enjoy resting with your new friend.

In the Desert

Imagine that you are camping in the desert.

You have a backpack with everything you need.

Feel the hot, dry air around you.

As you take a hike, animals come out of their hiding places.

You hear the sounds of lizards scurrying along the ground.

A roadrunner runs along the trail.

Small birds walk on the ground ahead of you.

As you get closer, you see that they are quail.

The feathers on their heads are shaped like question marks.

You stop and watch them for a while as they look for seeds to eat.

Now imagine that you find a group of desert plants.

There is a saguaro cactus, the tallest cactus you have ever seen.

A little bird called a cactus wren nests there.

There is also a flowering ocotillo plant.

It looks like a bunch of candlesticks with bright-red flowers for flames.

A hummingbird flies to one of the flowers to sip some nectar.

Its wings move quickly, but its body stays very still.

Now imagine that you hike back to your campground.

Take deep breaths and smell the desert air.

Watch the sun start to set and turn the desert beautiful colors.

Red and purple paint the sky.

Get into your sleeping bag and watch the day turn into night.

Enjoy relaxing and sleeping with the desert animals and plants.

Making Chocolate

NOTE: You may want to share some chocolate after reading this story. (Always check for allergies.) This is a good story to read during holidays when there are lots of tempting treats.

Imagine you are in the rainforest.

You see birds and monkeys.

They are eating fruits that are shaped like pods.

The birds and monkeys drop seeds on the ground of the forest as they eat the pods.

The animals leave, but the seeds are left there to grow.

Imagine that it rains and rains, and the seeds start to sprout.

Beautiful cacao trees grow, filled with smooth bright-green leaves.

Imagine that white flowers bloom on the trees.

Tiny flies buzz around the flowers and pollinate them.

Now the flowers slowly grow cacao pods, which the birds and monkeys love to eat.

Imagine picking the pods off the trees.

You open the pods, and you find seeds inside.

Imagine that you use a special machine to crack and cook the seeds.

Now you have a pot of gooey chocolate.

You can pour it into any shape you would like.

Imagine that once it is dry, you touch the chocolate and feel how smooth it is.

Now imagine that you take a deep breath in and out to smell the chocolate.

Look at the chocolate and see how shiny it is.

Now imagine that you taste the chocolate with only the tip of your tongue.

Imagine taking a small bite and letting it slowly melt in your mouth.

Enjoy how good this imaginary chocolate tastes.

Now think of the trees, flowers, insects, birds, and monkeys that helped you make this treat.

Imagine that you send them some love while enjoying the rest of your chocolate.

More Loving Kindness

NOTE: This story was originally printed in *Imaginations: Fun Relaxation Stories and Meditations for Kids*. We need more love in the world, and including this story is my way of spreading the love to as many people as possible!

Imagine that you are sending love to yourself.

Send yourself a valentine that says, "I love you."

Now tell each part of your body that you love it.

"I love you, feet."

"I love you, legs."

"I love you, belly."

"I love you, back."

"I love you, arms."

"I love you, face."

Notice how your body feels when you tell it that you love it.

Now think of someone you love very much—
maybe someone in your family or your best friend.

Send them some love.

Now think of someone who is mean or unfriendly.

Send this person some love, too.

Sometimes, people are mean because they don't feel loved.

So send this person some extra love.

Now think of all the people all over the world.

Send them some love, too.

Now imagine all of these people you've sent love to.

And now imagine that each of those people sends love back to you.

Feel their love coming back to you.

Additional Information and Resources

Looking for more information?

Visit BambinoYoga.com for additional products, resources, activities, and information about relaxation exercises for children.

Loved these stories and want more?

Check out *Imaginations: Fun Relaxation Stories and Meditations for Kids*. It won the San Diego Book Award for Children's Nonfiction! Or visit BambinoYoga.com to download additional stories.

Want to listen to relaxation stories?

Visit BambinoYoga.com to download audio files or purchase a CD.

Want to keep in touch?

Visit BambinoYoga.com and signup for the newsletter. You'll receive info about relaxation and yoga for kids, as well as contests, sales, and events. You can also like us at Facebook.com/BambinoYoga or follow @BambinoYoga on Twitter.

Want ideas for activities and arts and crafts that correspond with the relaxation stories?

Visit BambinoYoga.com/Activities or follow Pinterest.com/BambinoYoga.

Want to help spread the word about this book?

Email info@bambinoyoga.com to share how these stories have helped the children in your life or rate the book on Amazon.com, BN.com, or Goodreads.com to write about your experience.

Acknowledgements

Thank you to my family for your unending support and love. Laurie Clarke, thank you for testing out the stories in your classes, and Sun to Moon Yoga students, thank you for listening. Giselle Shardlow, thank you for your continued moral support. Megan Crowley and Chena Popper, thank you for reading and rereading. Angela Moorad, thank you for your feedback and enthusiasm. Gregg Stebben, thank you for letting me pick your brain and for helping spread the word. Donna Freeman, thank you for all you do for the kids yoga community. Stefanie Spangler Buswell, thank you for edits, suggestions, and grammar tips. Lorie DeWorken, thank you for adding so much beauty to this book. Addison, Hailey, Jayden, and Maddux, thank you for your yoga poses and smiles.

And a big thank you to my husband, Drew, for believing in me.
Your optimism and ability to relax are infectious. I love you.

Made in the USA
Coppell, TX
10 December 2020